John Hay

**Pike County Ballads and other Pieces**

John Hay

**Pike County Ballads and other Pieces**

ISBN/EAN: 9783743350489

Manufactured in Europe, USA, Canada, Australia, Japa

Cover: Foto ©ninafisch / pixelio.de

Manufactured and distributed by brebook publishing software (www.brebook.com)

John Hay

**Pike County Ballads and other Pieces**

# PIKE COUNTY BALLADS

AND

## OTHER PIECES.

By JOHN HAY.

JAMES R. OSGOOD AND COMPANY,
LATE TICKNOR & FIELDS, AND FIELDS, OSGOOD, & CO.
1871.

Entered according to Act of Congress, in the year 1871,
BY JOHN HAY,
in the Office of the Librarian of Congress, at Washington.

UNIVERSITY PRESS: WELCH, BIGELOW, & CO.
CAMBRIDGE.

## NOTE.

Some of the verses contained in this volume are now published for the first time. Those entitled "Banty Tim," "The Mystery of Gilgal," and "A Woman's Love," are reprinted from *Harper's Weekly;* "Northward" and "The Monks of Basle," from *Harper's Monthly.*

# CONTENTS.

## THE PIKE COUNTY BALLADS.

|  | PAGE |
|---|---|
| LITTLE BREECHES | 13 |
| JIM BLUDSO | 17 |
| BANTY TIM | 21 |
| THE MYSTERY OF GILGAL | 25 |

## WANDERLIEDER.

| | |
|---|---|
| SUNRISE IN THE PLACE DE LA CONCORDE | 31 |
| THE SPHINX OF THE TUILERIES | 39 |
| THE SURRENDER OF SPAIN | 42 |
| THE PRAYER OF THE ROMANS | 46 |
| THE CURSE OF HUNGARY | 49 |
| THE MONKS OF BASLE | 53 |
| THE ENCHANTED SHIRT | 59 |
| A WOMAN'S LOVE | 65 |
| ON PITZ LANGUARD | 68 |

## NEW AND OLD.

| | |
|---|---|
| In Church | 73 |
| Remorse | 75 |
| Esse Quam Videri | 77 |
| When the Boys come Home | 78 |
| Lèse-Amour | 81 |
| Northward | 84 |
| In the Firelight | 88 |
| After Heine | 92 |
| In a Graveyard | 93 |
| The Prairie | 95 |
| Centennial | 99 |
| A Winter Night | 105 |
| Student-Song | 106 |
| I. Cedar Mountain | 108 |
| II. Port Hudson | 110 |
| At Sunset | 111 |
| How it Happened | 115 |
| God's Vengeance | 118 |
| Too late | 120 |
| Love's Doubt | 123 |
| Lagrimas | 125 |
| Countess Jutta | 127 |

## CONTENTS.

| | |
|---|---|
| ON THE BLUFF | 129 |
| GOOD AND BAD LUCK | 131 |
| UNA | 132 |
| "THROUGH THE LONG DAYS AND YEARS" | 135 |
| A PHYLACTERY | 137 |
| BLONDINE | 139 |
| DISTICHES | 141 |
| REGARDANT | 143 |
| GUY OF THE TEMPLE | 146 |

# THE PIKE COUNTY BALLADS.

## LITTLE BREECHES.

I DON'T go much on religion,
    I never ain't had no show;
But I've got a middlin' tight grip, sir,
    On the handful o' things I know.
I don't pan out on the prophets
    And free-will, and that sort of thing,—
But I b'lieve in God and the angels,
    Ever sence one night last spring.

I come into town with some turnips,
    And my little Gabe come along,—
No four-year-old in the county
    Could beat him for pretty and strong,

Peart and chipper and sassy,
    Always ready to swear and fight,—
And I'd larnt him to chaw terbacker
    Jest to keep his milk-teeth white.

The snow come down like a blanket
    As I passed by Taggart's store;
I went in for a jug of molasses
    And left the team at the door.
They scared at something and started,—
    I heard one little squall,
And hell-to-split over the prairie
    Went team, Little Breeches and all.

Hell-to-split over the prairie!
    I was almost froze with skeer;
But we rousted up some torches,
    And sarched for 'em far and near.

At last we struck hosses and wagon,
    Snowed under a soft white mound,
Upsot, dead beat, — but of little Gabe
    No hide nor hair was found.

And here all hope soured on me,
    Of my fellow-critter's aid, —
I jest flopped down on my marrow-bones,
    Crotch-deep in the snow, and prayed.

    .    .    .    .

By this, the torches was played out,
    And me and Isrul Parr
Went off for some wood to a sheepfold
    That he said was somewhar thar.

We found it at last, and a little shed
    Where they shut up the lambs at night.

We looked in and seen them huddled thar,
    So warm and sleepy and white;
And THAR sot Little Breeches and chirped,
    As peart as ever you see,
"I want a chaw of terbacker,
    And that's what's the matter of me."

How did he git thar? Angels.
    He could never have walked in that storm.
They jest scooped down and toted him
    To whar it was safe and warm.
And I think that saving a little child,
    And bringing him to his own,
Is a derned sight better business
    Than loafing around The Throne.

# JIM BLUDSO,

## OF THE PRAIRIE BELLE.

WALL, no! I can't tell whar he lives,
    Becase he don't live, you see;
Leastways, he 's got out of the habit
    Of livin' like you and me.
Whar have you been for the last three year
    That you have n't heard folks tell
How Jimmy Bludso passed in his checks
    The night of the Prairie Belle?

He warn't no saint, — them engineers
    Is all pretty much alike, —

One wife in Natchez-under-the-Hill
    And another one here, in Pike;
A keerless man in his talk was Jim,
    And an awkward hand in a row,
But he never flunked, and he never lied, —
    I reckon he never knowed how.

And this was all the religion he had, —
    To treat his engine well;
Never be passed on the river
    To mind the pilot's bell;
And if ever the Prairie Belle took fire, —
    A thousand times he swore,
He'd hold her nozzle agin the bank
    Till the last soul got ashore.

All boats has their day on the Mississip,
    And her day come at last, —

The Movastar was a better boat,
  But the Belle she *would n't* be passed.
And so she come tearin' along that night —
  The oldest craft on the line —
With a nigger squat on her safety-valve,
  And her furnace crammed, rosin and pine.

The fire bust out as she clared the bar,
  And burnt a hole in the night,
And quick as a flash she turned, and made
  For that willer-bank on the right.
There was runnin' and cursin', but Jim yelled out,
  Over all the infernal roar,
"I'll hold her nozzle agin the bank
  Till the last galoot 's ashore."

Through the hot, black breath of the burnin' boat
  Jim Bludso's voice was heard,

And they all had trust in his cussedness,
    And knowed he would keep his word.
And, sure 's you 're born, they all got off
    Afore the smokestacks fell, —
And Bludso's ghost went up alone
    In the smoke of the Prairie Belle.

He were n't no saint, — but at jedgment
    I 'd run my chance with Jim,
'Longside of some pious gentlemen
    That would n't shook hands with him.
He seen his duty, a dead-sure thing, —
    And went for it thar and then;
And Christ ain't a-going to be too hard
    On a man that died for men.

# BANTY TIM.

### ARKS OF SERGEANT TILMON JOY TO THE WHITE MAN'S COMMITTEE OF SPUNKY POINT, ILLINOIS.)

I RECKON I git your drift, gents,—
   You 'low the boy sha' n't stay;
This is a white man's country;
   You 're Dimocrats, you say;
And whereas, and seein', and wherefore,
   The times bein' all out o' j'int,
The nigger has got to mosey
   From the limits o' Spunky P'int!


Le's reason the thing a minute:
   I 'm an old-fashioned Dimocrat too,

Though I laid my politics out o' the way
    For to keep till the war was through.
But I come back here, allowin'
    To vote as I used to do,
Though it gravels me like the devil to train
    Along o' sich fools as you.

Now dog my cats ef I kin see,
    In all the light of the day,
What you 've got to do with the question
    Ef Tim shill go or stay.
And furder than that I give notice,
    Ef one of you tetches the boy,
He kin check his trunks to a warmer clime
    Than he'll find in Illanoy.

Why, blame your hearts, jest hear me!
    You know that ungodly day

When our left struck Vicksburg Heights, how ripped
    And torn and tattered we lay.
When the rest retreated I stayed behind,
    Fur reasons sufficient to me, —
With a rib caved in, and a leg on a strike,
    I sprawled on that damned glacee.

Lord! how the hot sun went for us,
    And br'iled and blistered and burned!
How the Rebel bullets whizzed round us
    When a cuss in his death-grip turned!
Till along toward dusk I seen a thing
    I could n't believe for a spell:
That nigger — that Tim — was a crawlin' to me
    Through that fire-proof, gilt-edged hell!

The Rebels seen him as quick as me,
    And the bullets buzzed like bees;

But he jumped for me, and shouldered me,
  Though a shot brought him once to his knees;
But he staggered up, and packed me off,
  With a dozen stumbles and falls,
Till safe in our lines he drapped us both,
  His black hide riddled with balls.

So, my gentle gazelles, thar 's my answer,
  And here stays Banty Tim:
He trumped Death's ace for me that day,
  And I 'm not goin' back on him!
You may rezoloot till the cows come home,
  But ef one of you tetches the boy,
He 'll wrastle his hash to-night in hell,
  Or my name 's not Tilmon Joy!

# THE MYSTERY OF GILGAL.

THE darkest, strangest mystery
  I ever read, or heern, or see,
Is 'long of a drink at Taggart's Hall,—
  Tom Taggart's of Gilgal.

I 've heern the tale a thousand ways,
But never could git through the maze
That hangs around that queer day's doin's;
  But I 'll tell the yarn to youans.

Tom Taggart stood behind his bar,
The time was fall, the skies was far,
The neighbors round the counter drawed,
  And ca'mly drinked and jawed.

At last come Colonel Blood of Pike,
And old Jedge Phinn, permiscus-like,
And each, as he meandered in,
   Remarked, "A whisky-skin."

Tom mixed the beverage full and far,
And slammed it, smoking, on the bar.
Some says three fingers, some says two, —
   I'll leave the choice to you.

Phinn to the drink put forth his hand;
Blood drawed his knife, with accent bland,
"I ax yer parding, Mister Phinn —
   Jest drap that whisky-skin."

No man high-toneder could be found
Than old Jedge Phinn the country round.

## THE MYSTERY OF GILGAL.

Says he, "Young man, the tribe of Phinns
   Knows their own whisky-skins!"

He went for his 'leven-inch bowie-knife: —
"I tries to foller a Christian life;
But I'll drap a slice of liver or two,
   My bloomin' shrub, with you."

They carved in a way that all admired,
Tell Blood drawed iron at last, and fired.
It took Seth Bludso 'twixt the eyes,
   Which caused him great surprise.

Then coats went off, and all went in;
Shots and bad language swelled the din;
The short, sharp bark of Derringers,
   Like bull-pups, cheered the furse.

They piled the stiffs outside the door;
They made, I reckon, a cord or more.
Girls went that winter, as a rule,
  Alone to spellin'-school.

I've sarched in vain, from Dan to Beer-
Sheba, to make this mystery clear;
But I end with *hit* as I did begin,—
  WHO GOT THE WHISKY-SKIN?"

# WANDERLIEDER.

# SUNRISE IN THE PLACE DE LA CONCORDE.

(PARIS, AUGUST, 1865.)

I STAND at the break of day
   In the Champs Elysées.
The tremulous shafts of dawning
As they shoot o'er the Tuileries early,
Strike Luxor's cold gray spire,
And wild in the light of the morning
With their marble manes on fire,
Ramp the white Horses of Marly.


But the Place of Concord lies
Dead hushed 'neath the ashy skies.

And the Cities sit in council
With sleep in their wide stone eyes.
I see the mystic plain
Where the army of spectres slain
In the Emperor's life-long war
March on with unsounding tread
To trumpets whose voice is dead.
Their spectral chief still leads them, —
The ghostly flash of his sword
Like a comet through mist shines far, —
And the noiseless host is poured,
For the gendarme never heeds them,
Up the long dim road where thundered
The army of Italy onward
Through the great pale Arch of the Star!

The spectre army fades
Far up the glimmering hill,

But, vaguely lingering still,

A group of shuddering shades

Infects the pallid air,

Growing dimmer as day invades

The hush of the dusky square.

There is one that seems a King,

As if the ghost of a Crown

Still shadowed his jail-bleached hair;

I can hear the guillotine ring,

As its regicide note rang there,

When he laid his tired life down

And grew brave in his last despair.

And a woman frail and fair

Who weeps at leaving a world

Of love and revel and sin

In the vast Unknown to be hurled

(For life was wicked and sweet

With kings at her small white feet!)
And one, every inch a Queen,
In life and in death a Queen,
Whose blood baptized the place,
In the days of madness and fear, —
Her shade has never a peer
In majesty and grace.

Murdered and murderers swarm;
Slayers that slew and were slain,
Till the drenched place smoked with the rain
That poured in a torrent warm, —
Till red as the Riders of Edom
Were splashed the white garments of Freedom
With the wash of the horrible storm!

And Liberty's hands were not clean
In the day of her pride unchained,

Her royal hands were stained
With the life of a King and Queen;
And darker than that with the blood
Of the nameless brave and good
Whose blood in witness clings
More damning than Queens' and Kings'.

Has she not paid it dearly?
Chained, watching her chosen nation
Grinding late and early
In the mills of usurpation?
Have not her holy tears
Flowing through shameful years,
Washed the stains from her tortured hands?
We thought so when God's fresh breeze,
Blowing over the sleeping lands,
In 'Forty-Eight waked the world,

And the best of the kings was hurled
From that palace behind the trees.


As Freedom with eyes aglow
Smiled glad through her childbirth pain,
How was the mother to know
That her woe and travail were vain?
A smirking servant smiled
When she gave him her child to keep;
Did she know he would strangle the child
As it lay in his arms asleep?


Liberty's cruellest shame!
She is stunned and speechless yet.
In her grief and bloody sweat
Shall we make her trust her blame?
The treasure of 'Forty-Eight

A lurking jail-bird stole,

She can but watch and wait

As the swift sure seasons roll.


And when in God's good hour

Comes the time of the brave and true,

Freedom again shall rise

With a blaze in her awful eyes

That shall wither this robber-power

As the sun now dries the dew.

This Place shall roar with the voice

Of the glad triumphant people,

And the heavens be gay with the chimes

Ringing with jubilant noise

From every clamorous steeple

The coming of better times.

And the dawn of Freedom waking

Shall fling its splendors far

Like the day which now is breaking

On the great pale Arch of the Star,

And back o'er the town shall fly,

While the joy-bells wild are ringing,

To crown the Glory springing

From the Column of July!

# THE SPHINX OF THE TUILERIES.

OUT of the Latin Quarter
   I came to the lofty door
Where the two marble Sphinxes guard
   The Pavillon de Flore.
Two Cockneys stood by the gate, and one
   Observed, as they turned to go,
"No wonder He likes that sort of thing, —
   He's a Sphinx himself, you know."


I thought as I walked where the garden glowed
   In the sunset's level fire,
Of the Charlatan whom the Frenchmen loathe
   And the Cockneys all admire.

They call him a Sphinx, — it pleases him, —
    And if we narrowly read,
We will find some truth in the flunkey's praise,
    The man is a Sphinx indeed.

For the Sphinx with breast of woman
    And face so debonair
Had the sleek false paws of a lion,
    That could furtively seize and tear.
So far to the shoulders, — but if you took
    The Beast in reverse you would find
The ignoble form of a craven cur
    Was all that lay behind.

She lived by giving to simple folk
    A silly riddle to read,
And when they failed she drank their blood
    In cruel and ravenous greed.

it at last came one who knew her word,
And she perished in pain and shame, —
his bastard Sphinx leads the same base life
And his end will be the same.

For an Œdipus-People is coming fast
With swelled feet limping on,
they shout his true name once aloud
His false foul power is gone.
Afraid to fight and afraid to fly,
He cowers in an abject shiver;
The people will come to their own at last, —
God is not mocked forever.

# THE SURRENDER OF SPAIN.

### I.

LAND of unconquered Pelayo! land of the Cid Campeador!

Sea-girdled mother of men! Spain, name of glory and power;

Cradle of world-grasping Emperors, grave of the reckless invader,

How art thou fallen, my Spain! how art thou sunk at this hour!

### II.

Once thy magnanimous sons trod, victors, the portals of Asia,

Once the Pacific waves rushed, joyful thy banners to see;

For it was Trajan that carried the battle-flushed
    eagles to Dacia,
Cortés that planted thy flag fast by the uttermost
    sea.

### III.

Has thou forgotten those days illumined with glory
    and honor,
When the far isles of the sea thrilled to the tread
    of Castile?
When every land under Heaven was flecked by
    the shade of thy banner, —
When every beam of the sun flashed on thy con-
    quering steel?

### IV.

Then through red fields of slaughter, through death
    and defeat and disaster,
Still flared thy banner aloft, tattered, but free from
    a stain, —

Now to the upstart Savoyard thou bendest to beg
for a master!
How the red flush of her shame mars the proud
beauty of Spain!

v.

Has the red blood run cold that boiled by the
Xenil and Darro?
Are the high deeds of the sires sung to the children no more?
On the dun hills of the North hast thou heard of
no plough-boy Pizarro?
Roams no young swine-herd Cortés hid by the
Tagus' wild shore?

vi.

Once again does Hispania bend low to the yoke
of the stranger!
Once again will she rise, flinging her gyves in the
sea!

Princeling of Piedmont! unwitting thou weddest with doubt and with danger,
King over men who have learned all that it costs to be free.

# THE PRAYER OF THE ROMANS.

NOT done, but near its ending,
    Is the work that our eyes desired;
Not yet fulfilled, but near the goal,
    Is the hope that our worn hearts fired.
And on the Alban Mountains,
    Where the blushes of dawn increase,
We see the flash of the beautiful feet
    Of Freedom and of Peace!

How long were our fond dreams baffled! —
    Novara's sad mischance,
The Kaiser's sword and fetter-lock,
    And the traitor stab of France;

Till at last came glorious Venice,
   In storm and tempest home;
And now God maddens the greedy kings,
   And gives to her people Rome.

Lame Lion of Caprera!
   Red-shirts of the lost campaigns!
Not idly shed was the costly blood
   You poured from generous veins.
For the shame of Aspromonte,
   And the stain of Mentana's sod,
But forged the curse of kings that sprang
   From your breaking hearts to God!

We lift our souls to thee, O Lord
   Of Liberty and of Light!
Let not earth's kings pollute the work
   That was done in their despite;

Let not thy light be darkened
    In the shade of a sordid crown,
Nor the Piedmont swine devour the fruit
    Thou shook'st with an earthquake down!

Let the People come to their birthright,
    And crosier and crown pass away
Like phantasms that flit o'er the marshes
    At the glance of the clean, white day.
And then from the lava of Ætna
    To the ice of the Alps let there be
One freedom, one faith without fetters,
    One republic in Italy free!

# THE CURSE OF HUNGARY.

KING Saloman looked from his donjon bars,
    Where the Danube clamors through sedge and sand,
And he cursed with a curse his revolting land, —
With a king's deep curse of treason and wars.

He said: "May this false land know no truth!
    May the good hearts die and the bad ones flourish,
And a greed of glory but live to nourish
Envy and hate in its restless youth.

"In the barren soil may the ploughshare rust,
    While the sword grows bright with its fatal labor,

And blackens between each man and neighbor
The perilous cloud of a vague distrust!

"Be the noble idle, the peasant in thrall,
   And each to the other as unknown things,
   That with links of hatred and pride the kings
May forge firm fetters through each for all!

"May a king wrong them as they wronged their king!
   May he wring their hearts as they wrung mine,
   Till they pour their blood for his revels like wine,
And to women and monks their birthright fling!"

The mad king died; but the rushing river
   Still brawls by the spot where his donjon stands,
   And its swift waves sigh to the conscious sands
That the curse of King Saloman works forever.

For flowing by Pressbourg they heard the cheers
   Ring out from the leal and cheated hearts
   That were caught and chained by Theresa's arts, —
A man's cool head and a girl's hot tears!

And a star, scarce risen, they saw decline,
   Where Orsova's hills looked coldly down,
   As Kossuth buried the Iron Crown
And fled in the dark to the Turkish line.

And latest they saw in the summer glare
   The Magyar nobles in pomp arrayed,
   To shout as they saw, with his unfleshed blade,
A Hapsburg beating the harmless air.

But ever the same sad play they saw,
   The same weak worship of sword and crown,

The noble crushing the humble down,
And moulding Wrong to a monstrous Law.

The donjon stands by the turbid river,
    But Time is crumbling its battered towers;
    And the slow light withers a despot's powers,
And a mad king's curse is not forever!

## THE MONKS OF BASLE.

I TORE this weed from the rank, dark soil
 Where it grew in the monkish time,
I trimmed it close and set it again
 In a border of modern rhyme.

### I.

Long years ago, when the Devil was loose
 And faith was sorely tried,
Three monks of Basle went out to walk
 In the quiet eventide.

A breeze as pure as the breath of Heaven
 Blew fresh through the cloister-shades,

A sky as glad as the smile of Heaven
    Blushed rose o'er the minster-glades.

But scorning the lures of summer and sense,
    The monks passed on in their walk;
Their eyes were abased, their senses slept,
    Their souls were in their talk.

In the tough grim talk of the monkish days
    They hammered and slashed about, —
Dry husks of logic, — old scraps of creed, —
    And the cold gray dreams of doubt, —

And whether Just or Justified
    Was the Church's mystic Head, —
And whether the Bread was changed to God,
    Or God became the Bread.

But of human hearts outside their walls
　　They never paused to dream,
And they never thought of the love of God
　　That smiled in the twilight gleam.

II.

As these three monks went bickering on
　　By the foot of a spreading tree,
Out from its heart of verdurous gloom
　　A song burst wild and free, —

A wordless carol of life and love,
　　Of nature free and wild;
And the three monks paused in the evening shade,
　　Looked up at each other and smiled.

And tender and gay the bird sang on,
　　And cooed and whistled and trilled,

And the wasteful wealth of life and love
  From his happy heart was spilled.

The song had power on the grim old monks
  In the light of the rosy skies;
And as they listened the years rolled back,
  And tears came into their eyes.

The years rolled back and they were young,
  With the hearts and hopes of men,
They plucked the daisies and kissed the girls
  Of dear dead summers again.

### III.

But the eldest monk soon broke the spell;
  "'Tis sin and shame," quoth he,
"To be turned from talk of holy things
  By a bird's cry from a tree.

"Perchance the Enemy of Souls
  Hath come to tempt us so.
Let us try by the power of the Awful Word
  If it be he, or no!"


To Heaven the three monks raised their hands;
  "We charge thee, speak!" they said,
"By His dread Name who shall one day come
  To judge the quick and the dead, —


"Who art thou? Speak!" The bird laughed loud,
  "I am the Devil," he said.
The monks on their faces fell, the bird
  Away through the twilight sped.


A horror fell on those holy men,
  (The faithful legends say,)

And one by one from the face of earth
>They pined and vanished away.

### IV.

So goes the tale of the monkish books,
>The moral who runs may read,—

He has no ears for Nature's voice
>Whose soul is the slave of creed.

Not all in vain with beauty and love
>Has God the world adorned;

And he who Nature scorns and mocks,
>By Nature is mocked and scorned.

# THE ENCHANTED SHIRT.

Fytte y<sup>e</sup> Firste : *wherein it shall be shown how y<sup>e</sup> Truth is too mightie a Drugge for such as be of feeble temper.*

THE King was sick. His cheek was red
    And his eye was clear and bright;
He ate and drank with a kingly zest,
    And peacefully snored at night.

But he said he was sick, and a king should know,
    And doctors came by the score.
They did not cure him. He cut off their heads
    And sent to the schools for more.

At last two famous doctors came,
    And one was as poor as a rat,—

He had passed his life in studious toil,
  And never found time to grow fat.

The other had never looked in a book;
  His patients gave him no trouble,
If they recovered they paid him well,
  If they died their heirs paid double.

Together they looked at the royal tongue,
  As the King on his couch reclined;
In succession they thumped his august chest,
  But no trace of disease could find.

The old sage said, "You 're as sound as a nut."
  "Hang him up," roared the King in a gale, —
In a ten-knot gale of royal rage;
  The other leech grew a shade pale;

But he pensively rubbed his sagacious nose,
    And thus his prescription ran, —
*The King will be well, if he sleeps one night*
    *In the Shirt of a Happy Man.*


Fytte y<sup>e</sup> Seconde: *telleth of y<sup>e</sup> search for y<sup>e</sup> Shirte and how it was nighe founde but was notte, for reasons qu: are sayd or sung.*

Wide o'er the realm the couriers rode,
    And fast their horses ran,
And many they saw, and to many they spoke,
    But they found no Happy Man.


They found poor men who would fain be rich,
    And rich who thought they were poor;
And men who twisted their waists in stays,
    And women that shorthose wore.

They saw two men by the roadside sit,
    And both bemoaned their lot;
For one had buried his wife, he said,
    And the other one had not.

At last as they came to a village gate,
    A beggar lay whistling there;
He whistled and sang and laughed and rolled
    On the grass in the soft June air.

The weary couriers paused and looked
    At the scamp so blithe and gay;
And one of them said, "Heaven save you, friend!
    You seem to be happy to-day."

"O yes, fair sirs," the rascal laughed
    And his voice rang free and glad,

"An idle man has so much to do
    That he never has time to be sad."

"This is our man," the courier said;
    "Our luck has led us aright.
"I will give you a hundred ducats, friend,
    For the loan of your shirt to-night."

The merry blackguard lay back on the grass,
    And laughed till his face was black;
"I would do it, God wot," and he roared with the fun,
    "But I have n't a shirt to my back."

Fytte yᵉ Third: *Shewing how Hys Majestie yᵉ King came at last to sleepe in a Happie Man his Shirte.*

Each day to the King the reports came in
    Of his unsuccessful spies,

And the sad panorama of human woes
  Passed daily under his eyes.

And he grew ashamed of his useless life,
  And his maladies hatched in gloom;
He opened his windows and let the air
  Of the free heaven into his room.

And out he went in the world and toiled
  In his own appointed way;
And the people blessed him, the land was glad,
  And the King was well and gay.

# A WOMAN'S LOVE.

A SENTINEL angel sitting high in glory
Heard this shrill wail ring out from Purgatory:
"Have mercy, mighty angel, hear my story!

"I loved, — and, blind with passionate love, I fell.
Love brought me down to death, and death to Hell.
For God is just, and death for sin is well.

"I do not rage against his high decree,
Nor for myself do ask that grace shall be;
But for my love on earth who mourns for me.

"Great Spirit! Let me see my love again
And comfort him one hour, and I were fain
To pay a thousand years of fire and pain."

Then said the pitying angel, "Nay, repent
That wild vow! Look, the dial-finger's bent
Down to the last hour of thy punishment!"

But still she wailed, "I pray thee, let me go!
I cannot rise to peace and leave him so.
O, let me soothe him in his bitter woe!"

The brazen gates ground sullenly ajar,
And upward, joyous, like a rising star,
She rose and vanished in the ether far.

But soon adown the dying sunset sailing,
And like a wounded bird her pinions trailing,
She fluttered back, with broken-hearted wailing.

She sobbed, "I found him by the summer sea
Reclined, his head upon a maiden's knee, —
She curled his hair and kissed him. Woe is me!"

She wept, "Now let my punishment begin!
I have been fond and foolish. Let me in
To expiate my sorrow and my sin."

The angel answered, "Nay, sad soul, go higher!
To be deceived in your true heart's desire
Was bitterer than a thousand years of fire!"

## ON PITZ LANGUARD.

I STOOD on the top of Pitz Languard,
   And heard three voices whispering low,
Where the Alpine birds in their circling ward
   Made swift dark shadows upon the snow.

*First voice.*

I loved a girl with truth and pain,
   She loved me not. When she said good-by
She gave me a kiss to sting and stain
   My broken life to a rosy dye.

*Second voice.*

I loved a woman with love well tried, —
   And I swear I believe she loves me still.

But it was not I who stood by her side

When she answered the priest and said "I will."


*Third voice.*

I loved two girls, one fond, one shy,

    And I never divined which one loved me.

One married, and now, though I can't tell why,

    Of the four in the story I count but three.


The three weird voices whispered low

    Where the eagles swept in their circling ward;

But only one shadow scarred the snow

    As I clambered down from Pitz Languard.

# NEW AND OLD.

## IN CHURCH.

I NEVER may know the peace that sleeps
   In the light serene of your kindly eyes,
As true as the sentinel-star that keeps
   His circling tryst in the boreal skies.
Unknown to me is the faith they speak,
   And strange the flash of their silent prayer,
And the sacred joy that climbs your cheek
   To hang its fluttering signals there.

As the star-beams light on the tossing brine
   And hallow the surge of its wild unrest,
Your eyes in their tender pity shine
   To light the gloom of my doubting breast.

And hope springs up in their earnest gleams
  As a flower that leaps from the sun-kissed sod,
And I love their light as a beacon that beams
  To lead me trustingly up to God.


If ever I stand by the jasper sea,
  Whose bright waves flash in their awful pride,
The mingled strain of my thanks shall be
  That you have lived and that Christ has died.
By the life-stream glassing the Eden-flowers
  I will walk with you under shadowless skies,
And on forever through amaranth bowers
  I will follow the light of your guiding eyes.

# REMORSE.

SAD is the thought of sunniest days
    Of love and rapture perished,
And shine through memory's tearful haze
    The eyes once fondliest cherished.
Reproachful is the ghost of toys
    That charmed while life was wasted.
But saddest is the thought of joys
    That never yet were tasted.

Sad is the vague and tender dream
    Of dead love's lingering kisses,
To crushed hearts haloed by the gleam
    Of unreturning blisses;

Deep mourns the soul in anguished pride

   For the pitiless death that won them, —

But the saddest wail is for lips that died

   With the virgin dew upon them.

## ESSE QUAM VIDERI.

THE knightly legend of thy shield betrays
    The moral of thy life; a forecast wise,
  And that large honor that deceit defies,
Inspired thy fathers in the elder days,
Who decked thy scutcheon with that sturdy phrase,
    *To be rather than seem.* As eve's red skies
    Surpass the morning's rosy prophecies,
Thy life to that proud boast its answer pays,
Scorning thy faith and purpose to defend
    The ever-mutable multitude at last
    Will hail the power they did not comprehend, —
Thy fame will broaden through the centuries;
    As, storm and billowy tumult overpast,
    The moon rules calmly o'er the conquered seas.

## WHEN THE BOYS COME HOME.

There's a happy time coming,
    When the boys come home.
There's a glorious day coming,
    When the boys come home.
We will end the dreadful story
Of this treason dark and gory
In a sunburst of glory,
    When the boys come home.

The day will seem brighter
    When the boys come home,
For our hearts will be lighter
    When the boys come home.

Wives and sweethearts will press them
In their arms and caress them,
And pray God to bless them,
   When the boys come home.

The thinned ranks will be proudest
   When the boys come home,
And their cheer will ring the loudest
   When the boys come home.
The full ranks will be shattered,
And the bright arms will be battered,
And the battle-standards tattered,
   When the boys come home.

Their bayonets may be rusty,
   When the boys come home,
And their uniforms dusty,
   When the boys come home.

But all shall see the traces
Of battle's royal graces,
In the brown and bearded faces,
  When the boys come home.


Our love shall go to meet them,
  When the boys come home,
To bless them and to greet them,
  When the boys come home;
And the fame of their endeavor
Time and change shall not dissever
From the nation's heart forever,
  When the boys come home.

## LÈSE-AMOUR.

HOW well my heart remembers
    Beside these camp-fire embers
The eyes that smiled so far away, —
    The joy that was November's.

    Her voice to laughter moving,
    So merrily reproving, —
We wandered through the autumn woods,
    And neither thought of loving.

    The hills with light were glowing,
    The waves in joy were flowing, —
It was not to the clouded sun
    The day's delight was owing.

Though through the brown leaves straying,
    Our lives seemed gone a-Maying;
We knew not Love was with us there,
    No look nor tone betraying.

How unbelief still misses
    The best of being's blisses!
Our parting saw the first and last
    Of love's imagined kisses.

Now 'mid these scenes the drearest
    I dream of her, the dearest, —
Whose eyes outshine the Southern stars,
    So far, and yet the nearest.

And Love, so gayly taunted,
    Who died, no welcome granted,

Comes to me now, a pallid ghost,

By whom my life is haunted.


With bonds I may not sever,

He binds my heart forever,

And leads me where we murdered him, —

The Hill beside the River.

CAMP SHAW, FLORIDA, February, 1864.

# NORTHWARD.

UNDER the high unclouded sun
   That makes the ship and shadow one,
I sail away as from the fort
Booms sullenly the noonday gun.

The odorous airs blow thin and fine,
The sparkling waves like emeralds shine,
   The lustre of the coral reefs
Gleams whitely through the tepid brine.

And glitters o'er the liquid miles
The jewelled ring of verdant isles,
   Where generous Nature holds her court
Of ripened bloom and sunny smiles.

Encinctured by the faithful seas
Inviolate gardens load the breeze,
  Where flaunt like giant-warders' plumes
The pennants of the cocoa-trees.

Enthroned in light and bathed in balm,
In lonely majesty the Palm
  Blesses the isles with waving hands, —
High-Priest of the eternal Calm.

Yet Northward with an equal mind
I steer my course, and leave behind
  The rapture of the Southern skies, —
The wooing of the Southern wind.

For here o'er Nature's wanton bloom
Falls far and near the shade of gloom,

Cast from the hovering vulture-wings
Of one dark thought of woe and doom.

I know that in the snow-white pines
The brave Norse fire of freedom shines,
   And fain for this I leave the land
Where endless summer pranks the vines.

O strong, free North, so wise and brave!
O South, too lovely for a slave!
   Why read ye not the changeless truth,—
The free can conquer but to save?

May God upon these shining sands
Send Love and Victory clasping hands,
   And Freedom's banners wave in peace
Forever o'er the rescued lands!

And here, in that triumphant hour,
Shall yielding Beauty wed with Power;
 And blushing earth and smiling sea
In dalliance deck the bridal bower.

# IN THE FIRELIGHT.

MY dear wife sits beside the fire
    With folded hands and dreaming eyes,
Watching the restless flames aspire,
    And wrapped in thralling memories.
I mark the fitful firelight fling
    Its warm caresses on her brow,
    And kiss her hands' unmelting snow,
And glisten on her wedding-ring.

The proud free head that crowns so well
    The neck superb, whose outlines glide
Into the bosom's perfect swell
    Soft-billowed by its peaceful tide,

The cheek's faint flush, the lip's red glow,
   The gracious charm her beauty wears,
   Fill my fond eyes with tender tears
As in the days of long ago.

Days long ago, when in her eyes
   The only heaven I cared for lay,
When from our thoughtless Paradise
   All care and toil dwelt far away;
When Hope in wayward fancies throve,
   And rioted in secret sweets,
   Beguiled by Passion's dear deceits, —
The mysteries of maiden love.

One year had passed since first my sight
   Was gladdened by her girlish charms,
When on a rapturous summer night
   I clasped her in possessing arms.

And now ten years have rolled away,
    And left such blessings as their dower,
    I owe her tenfold at this hour
The love that lit our wedding-day.

For now, vague-hovering o'er her form,
    My fancy sees, by love refined,
A warmer and a dearer charm
    By wedlock's mystic hands intwined, —
A golden coil of wifely cares
    That years have forged, the loving joy
    That guards the curly-headed boy
Asleep an hour ago up stairs.

A fair young mother, pure as fair,
    A matron heart and virgin soul!
The flickering light that crowns her hair
    Seems like a saintly aureole.

## IN THE FIRELIGHT.

A tender sense upon me falls
    That joy unmerited is mine,
    And in this pleasant twilight shine
My perfect bliss myself appalls.


Come back! my darling, strayed so far
    Into the realm of fantasy, —
Let thy dear face shine like a star
    In love-light beaming over me.
My melting soul is jealous, sweet,
    Of thy long silence' drear eclipse,
    O kiss me back with living lips
To life, love, lying at thy feet!

# AFTER HEINE.

WHEN I look on thee and feel how dear,
    How pure, and how fair thou art,
Into my eyes there steals a tear,
And a shadow mingled of love and fear
    Creeps slowly over my heart.

And my very hands feel as if they would lay
    Themselves on thy fair young head,
And pray the good God to keep thee alway
As good and lovely, as pure and gay,—
    When I and my wild love are dead.

# IN A GRAVEYARD.

IN the dewy depths of the graveyard
   I lie in the tangled grass,
And watch, in the sea of azure,
   The white cloud-islands pass.

The birds in the rustling branches
   Sing gayly overhead;
Gray stones like sentinel spectres
   Are guarding the silent dead.

The early flowers sleep shaded
   In the cool green noonday glooms;
The broken light falls shuddering
   On the cold white face of the tombs.

Without, the world is smiling
In the infinite love of God,
But the sunlight fails and falters
When it falls on the churchyard sod.

On me the joyous rapture
Of a heart's first love is shed,
But it falls on my heart as coldly
As sunlight on the dead.

# THE PRAIRIE.

The skies are blue above my head,
    The prairie green below,
And flickering o'er the tufted grass
    The shifting shadows go,
Vague-sailing, where the feathery clouds
    Fleck white the tranquil skies,
Black javelins darting where aloft
    The whirring pheasant flies.

A glimmering plain in drowsy trance
    The dim horizon bounds,
Where all the air is resonant
    With sleepy summer sounds,—

The life that sings among the flowers,
    The lisping of the breeze,
The hot cicala's sultry cry,
    The murmurous dream of bees.

The butterfly — a flying flower —
    Wheels swift in flashing rings,
And flutters round his quiet kin,
    With brave flame-mottled wings.

The wild Pinks burst in crimson fire,
    The Phlox' bright clusters shine,
And Prairie-Cups are swinging free
    To spill their airy wine.

And lavishly beneath the sun,
    In liberal splendor rolled,
The Fennel fills the dipping plain
    With floods of flowery gold;

And widely weaves the Iron-Weed
    A woof of purple dyes
Where Autumn's royal feet may tread
    When bankrupt Summer flies.

In verdurous tumult far away
    The prairie-billows gleam,
Upon their crests in blessing rests
    The noontide's gracious beam.
Low quivering vapors steaming dim
    The level splendors break
Where languid Lilies deck the rim
    Of some land-circled lake.

Far in the East like low-hung clouds
    The waving woodlands lie;
Far in the West the glowing plain
    Melts warmly in the sky

No accent wounds the reverent air,

No footprint dints the sod, —

Lone in the light the prairie lies,

Rapt in a dream of God.

## CENTENNIAL.

A HUNDRED times the bells of Brown
   Have rung to sleep the idle summers,
And still to-day clangs clamoring down
   A greeting to the welcome comers.

And far, like waves of morning, pours
   Her call, in airy ripples breaking,
And wanders to the farthest shores,
   Her children's drowsy hearts awaking.

The wild vibration floats along,
   O'er heart-strings tense its magic plying,
And wakes in every breast its song
   Of love and gratitude undying.

My heart to meet the summons leaps
    At limit of its straining tether,
Where the fresh western sunlight steeps
    In golden flame the prairie heather.

And others, happier, rise and fare
    To pass within the hallowed portal,
And see the glory shining there
    Shrined in her steadfast eyes immortal.

What though their eyes be dim and dull,
    Their heads be white in reverend blossom;
Our mother's smile is beautiful
    As when she bore them on her bosom!

Her heavenly forehead bears no line
    Of Time's iconoclastic fingers,

But o'er her form the grace divine
  Of deathless youth and wisdom lingers.

We fade and pass, grow faint and old,
  Till youth and joy and hope are banished,
And still her beauty seems to fold
  The sum of all the glory vanished.

As while Tithonus faltered on
  The threshold of the Olympian dawnings,
Aurora's front eternal shone
  With lustre of the myriad mornings.

So joys that slip like dead leaves down,
  And hopes burnt out that die in ashes,
Rise restless from their graves to crown
  Our mother's brow with fadeless flashes.

And lives wrapped in tradition's mist
    These honored halls to-day are haunting,
And lips by lips long withered kissed
    The sagas of the past are chanting.

Scornful of absence' envious bar
    BROWN smiles upon the mystic meeting
Of those her sons, who, sundered far,
    In brotherhood of heart are greeting;

Her wayward children wandering on
    Where setting stars are lowly burning,
But still in worship toward the dawn
    That gilds their souls' dear Mecca turning;

Or those who, armed for God's own fight,
    Stand by his word through fire and slaughter,

Or bear our banner's starry light
 Far-flashing through the Gulf's blue water.

For where one strikes for light and truth
 The right to aid, the wrong redressing,
The mother of his spirit's youth
 Sheds o'er his soul her silent blessing.

She gained her crown a gem of flame
 When KNEASS fell dead in victory gory;
New splendor blazed upon her name
 When IVES' young life went out in glory!

Thus bright forever may she keep
 Her fires of tolerant Freedom burning,
Till War's red eyes are charmed to sleep
 And bells ring home the boys returning.

And may she shed her radiant truth
In largess on ingenuous comers,
And hold the bloom of gracious youth
Through many a hundred tranquil summers!

# A WINTER NIGHT.

THE winter wind is raving fierce and shrill
    And chides with angry moan the frosty skies,
  The white stars gaze with sleepless Gorgon eyes
That freeze the earth in terror fixed and still.
We reck not of the wild night's gloom and chill,
    Housed from its rage, dear friend; and fancy flies,
    Lured by the hand of beckoning memories,
Back to those summer evenings on the hill
Where we together watched the sun go down
    Beyond the gold-washed uplands, while his fires
    Touched into glittering life the vanes and spires
Piercing the purpling mists that veiled the town.
  The wintry night thy voice and eyes beguile,
  Till wake the sleeping summers in thy smile.

# STUDENT-SONG.

WHEN Youth's warm heart beats high, my friend,
    And Youth's blue sky is bright,
And shines in Youth's clear eye, my friend,
    Love's early dawning light,
Let the free soul spurn care's control,
    And while the glad days shine,
We'll use their beams for Youth's gay dreams
    Of Love and Song and Wine.

Let not the bigot's frown, my friend,
    O'ercast thy brow with gloom,
For Autumn's sober brown, my friend,
    Shall follow Summer's bloom.

Let smiles and sighs and loving eyes
 In changeful beauty shine,
And shed their beams on Youth's gay dreams
 Of Love and Song and Wine.


For in the weary years, my friend,
 That stretched before us lie,
There 'll be enough of tears, my friend,
 To dim the brightest eye.
So let them wait, and laugh at fate,
 While Youth's sweet moments shine, —
Till memory gleams with golden dreams
 Of Love and Song and Wine.

## I. CEDAR MOUNTAIN.

IT was a rare good fortune to our arms,
   That, when the flushed foe through the mountains poured,
He found there by the rushing river-ford
One whose calm soul was stranger to alarms.
Serene amid the conflict's fiery harms,
   Master of fate, of his own spirit lord,
   Like that stout knight on whose firm mail the sword
Clashed shivering, glanced, nor burst the faery charms.
An Iron Man! in happier days that name
   Hailed him the peaceful champion of the North;
   And now the faithful years have blazoned forth

Its splendid prophecy in the battle's flame.

Twice-fortunate brow where grandly darkening down

The warrior-laurel shades the civic crown!

## II. PORT HUDSON.

AGAIN thy name the listening nation thrills!
    Coy Victory, won with war's importunate roar,
    Crowns thy rough wooing by the Western shore,
As once amid Virginia's breezy hills.
The mighty thunder of thy triumph fills
    The guilty South; its stealthy echoes pour
    Through treason-haunted regions, evermore
Waking wild whispers, and the nameless ills
Of bondage wasting with the potent light
    Of hope; for slavery death-stricken lies
    Where the vague fame of thy black warrior flies.
The bloody shapes that troubled the dead night
Of woe and war fade as the dawn grows bright,
    And day comes flushing up the tranquil skies.

## AT SUNSET.

INTO the grave of twilight
　　The red gleam fades away,
And the westering clouds grow sombre
　　With love of the dying day.
　　　　In the eve's soft flush
　　　　The gloaming's hush
　　Comes down on the rippled bay.


The towering hills stand saintly,
　　Each grand head halo-crowned,
And the vagrant shadows wander
　　To the slope of the grassy ground;
　　　　The languid breeze

Stirs not the trees
In the trancing twilight bound.

Now climbs the vanishing glimmer
To the mountain's umber crest,
The sunset's molten glory
Glows gold on the water's breast;
From Heaven's dim crown
Comes kindly down
The gracious spirit of rest.

The cordial soul of the sunset
Steals warm to my heart like wine,
My weary eyes look fondly
Far over the glowing brine;
And tenderly beams
In a mist of dreams
A joy that shall never be mine.

## AT SUNSET.

Sweet eyes whose proud dark splendor
  Is melted in love's soft beams,
The still queen-features glorious
  In the dawn of love's first gleams;
    Imperial lips
    In the dear eclipse
  Of passion's tropical dreams.

Dear Heaven! to hear the ·rose-lips
  Breathe falteringly my name,
To see the soft cheek flushing
  With the joy of maiden shame!
    And feel the bliss
    Of her passionate kiss
  Touch every vein to flame.

And my saddened love seems lovelier
  In the tender evening shine,

And a vague hope wakes that a love so true
With an answering love must twine.
That Heaven will bend
And the love descend,
For ever and ever mine!

Fades the fair light from the waters, —
Cold shimmer the stars above, —
The desolate night-wind shudders
Through the dusk of the gloomy grove.
The vision is gone, —
I sit alone
With darkness and silence and love.

## HOW IT HAPPENED.

I PRAY you, pardon me, Elsie,
   And smile that frown away
That dims the light of your lovely face
   As a thunder-cloud the day.
I really could not help it, —
   Before I thought, 't was done, —
And those great gray eyes flashed bright and cold,
   Like an icicle in the sun.

I was thinking of the summers
   When we were boys and girls,
And wandered in the blossoming woods,
   And the gay winds romped with your curls.

And you seemed to me the same little girl
   I kissed in the alder-path,
I kissed the little girl's lips, and alas!
   I have roused a woman's wrath.

There is not so much to pardon, —
   For why were your lips so red?
The blond hair fell in a shower of gold
   From the proud, provoking head.
And the beauty that flashed from the splendid
   And played round the tender mouth,
Rushed over my soul like a warm sweet wind
   That blows from the fragrant south.

And where, after all, is the harm done?
   I believe we were made to be gay,
And all of youth not given to love
   Is vainly squandered away.

And strewn through life's low labors,
  Like gold in the desert sands,
Are love's swift kisses and sighs and vows
  And the clasp of clinging hands.


And when you are old and lonely,
  In Memory's magic shine
You will see on your thin and wasting hands,
  Like gems, these kisses of mine.
And when you muse at evening
  At the sound of some vanished name,
The ghost of my kisses shall touch your lips
  And kindle your heart to flame.

# GOD'S VENGEANCE.

Saith the Lord, "Vengeance is mine;
   I will repay," saith the Lord;
Ours be the anger divine,
   Lit by the flash of his word.

How shall his vengeance be done?
   How, when his purpose is clear?
Must he come down from his throne?
   Hath he no instruments here?

Sleep not in imbecile trust
   Waiting for God to begin,

While, growing strong in the dust,
    Rests the bruised serpent of sin.


Right and Wrong, — both cannot live
    Death-grappled. Which shall we see?
Strike! only Justice can give
    Safety to all that shall be.


Shame! to stand paltering thus,
    Tricked by the balancing odds;
Strike! God is waiting for us!
    Strike! for the vengeance is God's.

## TOO LATE.

Had we but met in other days,
    Had we but loved in other ways,
Another light and hope had shone
    On your life and my own.

In sweet but hopeless reveries
I fancy how your wistful eyes
Had saved me, had I known their power
    In fate's imperious hour;

How loving you, beloved of God,
And following you, the path I trod
Had led me, through your love and prayers,
    To God's love unawares:

And how our beings joined as one
Had passed through checkered shade and sun,
Until the earth our lives had given,
    With little change, to heaven.

God knows why this was not to be.
You bloomed from childhood far from me,
The sunshine of the favored place
    That knew your youth and grace.

And when your eyes, so fair and free,
In fearless beauty beamed on me,
I knew the fatal die was thrown,
    My choice in life was gone.

And still with wild and tender art
Your child-love touched my torpid heart,

Gilding the blackness where it fell,
    Like sunlight over hell.

In vain, in vain! my choice was gone!
Better to struggle on alone
Than blot your pure life's blameless shine
    With cloudy stains of mine.

A vague regret, a troubled prayer,
And then the future vast and fair
Will tempt your young and eager eyes
    With all its glad surprise.

And I shall watch you, safe and far,
As some late traveller eyes a star
Wheeling beyond his desert sands
    To gladden happier lands.

## LOVE'S DOUBT.

'TIS love that blinds my heart and eyes, —
   I sometimes say in doubting dreams, —
   The face that near me perfect seems
Cold Memory paints in fainter dyes.

'T was but love's dazzled eyes — I say —
   That made her seem so strangely bright;
   The face I worshipped yesternight,
I dread to meet it changed to-day.

As, when dies out some song's refrain,
   And leaves your eyes in happy tears,
   Awake the same fond idle fears, —
It cannot sound so sweet again.

You wait and say with vague annoy,
"It will not sound so sweet again,"
Until comes back the wild refrain
That floods your soul with treble joy.

So when I see my love again
Fades the unquiet doubt away,
While shines her beauty like the day
Over my happy heart and brain.

And in that face I see no more
The fancied faults I idly dreamed,
But all the charms that fairest seemed,
I find them, fairer than before.

## LAGRIMAS.

GOD send me tears !
Loose the fierce band that binds my tired brain,
Give me the melting heart of other years,
    And let me weep again !

    Before me pass
The shapes of things inexorably true.
Gone is the sparkle of transforming dew
    From every blade of grass.

    In life's high noon
Aimless I stand, my promised task undone,
And raise my hot eyes to the angry sun
    That will go down too soon.

Turned into gall
Are the sweet joys of childhood's sunny reign;
And memory is a torture, love a chain
That binds my life in thrall.

And childhood's pain
Could to me now the purest rapture yield;
I pray for tears as in his parching field
The husbandman for rain.

We pray in vain!
The sullen sky flings down its blaze of brass;
The joys of life all scorched and withering pass;
I shall not weep again.

# COUNTESS JUTTA.

### FROM THE GERMAN OF HEINRICH HEINE.

THE Countess Jutta passed over the Rhine
In a light canoe by the moon's pale shine.
The handmaid rows and the Countess speaks:
"Seest thou not there where the water breaks
  Seven corpses swim
  In the moonlight dim?
So sorrowful swim the dead!

"They were seven knights full of fire and youth,
They sank on my heart and swore me truth.
I trusted them; but for Truth's sweet sake,

Lest they should be tempted their oaths to break,
  I had them bound,
   And tenderly drowned!
So sorrowful swim the dead!"


The merry Countess laughed outright!
It rang so wild in the startled night!
Up to the waist the dead men rise
And stretch lean fingers to the skies.
  They nod and stare
   With a glassy glare!
So sorrowful swim the dead!

## ON THE BLUFF.

O GRANDLY flowing River!
O silver-gliding River!
Thy springing willows shiver
In the sunset as of old;
They shiver in the silence
Of the willow-whitened islands,
While the sun-bars and the sand-bars
Fill air and wave with gold.


O gay, oblivious River!
O sunset-kindled River!
Do you remember ever
The eyes and skies so blue

On a summer day that shone here,
When we were all alone here,
And the blue eyes were too wise
   To speak the love they knew?

O stern impassive River!
O still unanswering River!
The shivering willows quiver
   As the night-winds moan and rave.
From the past a voice is calling,
From heaven a star is falling,
And dew swells in the bluebells
   Above her hillside grave.

# GOOD AND BAD LUCK.

#### FROM THE GERMAN OF HEINE.

GOOD LUCK is the gayest of all gay girls,
    Long in one place she will not stay,
Back from your brow she strokes the curls,
    Kisses you quick and flies away.

But Madame Bad Luck soberly comes
    And stays,—no fancy has she for flitting,—
Snatches of true love-songs she hums,
    And sits by your bed, and brings her knitting.

## UNA.

IN the whole wide world there was but one,
    Others for others, but she was mine,
The one fair woman beneath the sun.

From her gold-flax curls' most marvellous shine
Down to the lithe and delicate feet
There was not a curve nor a waving line

But moved in a harmony firm and sweet
With all of passion my life could know.
By knowledge perfect and faith complete

I was bound to her, — as the planets go
Adoring around their central star,
Free, but united for weal or woe.

She was so near and Heaven so far —
She grew my heaven and law and fate
Rounding my life with a mystic bar

No thought beyond could violate.
Our love to fulness in silence nursed
Grew calm as morning, when through the gate

Of the glimmering East the sun has burst,
With his hot life filling the waiting air.
She kissed me once, — that last and first

Of her maiden kisses was placid as prayer.
Against all comers I sat with lance
In rest, and, drunk with my joy, I sware

Defiance and scorn to the world's worst chance.
In vain! for soon unhorsed I lay
At the feet of the strong god Circumstance —

And never again shall break the day,
And never again shall fall the night
That shall light me, or shield me, on my way

To the presence of my sad soul's delight.
Her dead love comes like a passionate ghost
To mourn the Body it held so light,

And Fate, like a hound with a purpose lost,
Goes round bewildered with shame and fright.

THROUGH the long days and years
 What will my loved one be,
  Parted from me?
Through the long days and years.


Always as then she was
 Loveliest, brightest, best,
  Blessing and blest, —
Always as then she was.


Never on earth again
 Shall I before her stand,
  Touch lip or hand, —
Never on earth again.

But while my darling lives
    Peaceful I journey on,
        Not quite alone,
Not while my darling lives.

## A PHYLACTERY.

WISE men I hold those rakes of old
   Who, as we read in antique story,
When lyres were struck and wine was poured,
Set the white Death's Head on the board —
   Memento mori.

Love well! love truly! and love fast!
   True love evades the dilatory.
Life's bloom flares like a meteor past;
A joy so dazzling cannot last —
   Memento mori.

Stop not to pluck the leaves of bay
   That greenly deck the path of glory,

The wreath will wither if you stay,
So pass along your earnest way —
    Memento mori.

Hear but not heed, though wild and shrill,
    The cries of faction transitory;
Cleave to *your* good, eschew *your* ill,
A Hundred Years and all is still —
    Memento mori.

When Old Age comes with muffled drums,
    That beat to sleep our tired life's story,
On thoughts of dying, (Rest is good!)
Like old snakes coiled i' the sun, we brood —
    Memento mori.

## BLONDINE.

I WANDERED through a careless world,
  Deceived when not deceiving,
And never gave an idle heart
  The rapture of believing.

The smiles, the sighs, the glancing eyes,
  Of many hundred comers
Swept by me, light as rose-leaves blown
  From long-forgotten summers.


But never eyes so deep and bright
  And loyal in their seeming,
And never smiles so full of light
  Have shone upon my dreaming.

The looks and lips so gay and wise,
> The thousand charms that wreathe them,
— Almost I dare believe that truth
> Is safely shrined beneath them.

Ah! do they shine, those eyes of thine,
> But for our own misleading?
The fresh young smile, so pure and fine,
> Does it but mock our reading?
Then faith is fled, and trust is dead,
> And unbelief grows duty,
If fraud can wield the triple arm
> Of youth and wit and beauty.

# DISTICHES.

### I.

WISELY a woman prefers to a lover a man who neglects her.
This one may love her some day, some day the lover will not.

### II.

There are three species of creatures who when they seem coming are going,
When they seem going they come: Diplomates, women, and crabs.

### III.

Pleasures too hastily tasted grow sweeter in fond recollection,

As the pomegranate plucked green ripens far over the sea.

### IV.

As the meek beasts in the Garden came flocking for Adam to name them,
Men for a title to-day crawl to the feet of a king.

### V.

What is a first love worth, except to prepare for a second?
What does the second love bring? Only regret for the first.

### VI.

Health was wooed by the Romans in groves of the laurel and myrtle.
Happy and long are the lives brightened by glory and love.

## REGARDANT.

AS I lay at your feet that afternoon,
    Little we spoke,— you sat and mused,
Humming a sweet old-fashioned tune,

And I worshipped you, with a sense confused
Of the good time gone and the bad on the way,
While my hungry eyes your face perused

To catch and brand on my soul for aye
The subtle smile which had grown my doom.
Drinking sweet poison hushed I lay

Till the sunset shimmered athwart the room.
I rose to go. You stood so fair
And dim in the dead day's tender gloom:

All at once, or ever I was aware,

Flashed from you on me a warm strong wave

Of passion and power; in the silence there

I fell on my knees, like a lover, or slave,

With my wild hands clasping your slender waist;

And my lips, with a sudden frenzy brave,

A madman's kiss on your girdle pressed,

And I felt your calm heart's quickening beat,

And your soft hands on me one instant rest.

And if God had loved me, how endlessly sweet

Had he let my heart in its rapture burst,

And throb its last at your firm small feet!

And when I was forth, I shuddered at first

At my imminent bliss. As a soul in pain,

Treading his desolate path accursed,

Looks back and dreams through his tears' dim
 rain
That by Heaven's wide gate the angels smile,
Relenting, and beckon him back again,

And goes on, thrice damned by that devil's wile,—
So sometimes burns in my weary brain
The thought that you loved me all the while.

# GUY OF THE TEMPLE.

DOWN the dim West slow fails the stricken sun,
And from his hot face fades the crimson flush
Veiled in death's herald-shadows sick and gray.
Silent and dark the sombre valley lies
Forgotten; happy in the late fond beams
Glimmer the constant waves of Galilee.
Afar, below, in airy music ring
The bugles of my host; the column halts,
A wearied serpent glittering in the vale,
Where rising mist-like gleam the tented camps.

Pitch my pavilion here, where its high cross
May catch the last light lingering on the hill.

The savage shadows, struggling by the shore,
Have conquered in the valley ; inch by inch
The vanquished light fights bravely to these crags
To perish glorious in the sunset fire ;
Even as our hunted Cause so pressed and torn
In Syrian valleys, and the trampled marge
Of consecrated streams, displays at last
Its narrowing glories from these steadfast walls.
Here in God's name we stand, and brighter far
Shines the stern virtue of my martyr-host
Through these invidious fortunes, than of old,
When the still sunshine glintèd on their helms,
And dallying breezes woke their bridle-bells
To tinkling music by the reedy shore
Of calm Tiberias, where our angry Lord,
Wroth at the deadly sin that cursed our camp,
Denied and blinded us, and gave us up

To the avenging sword of Saladin.
Yet would he not permit his truth to sink
To utter loss amid that foundering fight,
But led us, scarred and shattered from the spoil
Of Paynim rage, the desert's thirsty death,
To where beneath the sheltering crags we prayed
And rested and grew strong.  Heroes and saints
To alien peoples shall they be, my brave
And patient warriors; for in their stout hearts
God's spirit dwells forever, and their hands
Are swift to do his service on his foes.
The swelling music of their vesper-hymn
Is rising fragrant from the shadowed vale
Familiar to the welcoming gates of heaven.

*Mother of God! as evening falls*
    *Upon the silent sea,*

*And shadows veil the mountain walls,*
   *We lift our souls to thee!*
*From lurking perils of the night,*
   *The desert's hidden harms,*
*From plagues that waste, from blasts that smite,*
   *Defend thy men-at-arms!*


Ay! Heaven keep them! and ye angel-hosts
That wait with fluttering plumes around the great
White throne of God, guard them from scathe and
   harm!
For in your starry records never shone
The memory of desert so great as theirs.
I hold not first, though peerless else on earth,
That knightly valor, born of gentle blood
And war's long tutelage, which hath made their
   name

Blaze like a baleful planet o'er these lands;
Firm seat in saddle, lance unmoved, a hand
Wedding the hilt with death's persistent grasp;
One-minded rush in fight that naught can stay.
Not these the highest, though I scorn not these,
But rather offer Heaven with humble heart
The deeds that heaven hath given us arms to do.
For when God's smile was with us we were strong
To go like sudden lightning to our mark:
As on that summer day when Saladin —
Passing in scorn our host at Antioch,
Who spent the days in revel, and shamed the stars
With nightly scandal — came with all his host,
Its gay battalia brave with saffron silks,
Flaunting the banners of the Caliphate
Beneath the walls of fair Jerusalem:
And white and shaking came the Leper-King,

Great Baldwin's blasted scion, and Tripoli
And I, and twenty score of Temple Knights,
To meet the myriads marshalled by the bright
Untarnished flower of Eastern chivalry;
A moment paused with level-fronting spears
And moveless helms before that shining host,
Whose gay attire abashed the morning light,
And then struck spur and charged, while from the mass
Of rushing terror burst the awful cry,
*God and the Temple!* As the avalanche slides
Down Alpine slopes, precipitous, cold and dark,
Unpitying and unwrathful, grinds and crushes
The mountain violets and the valley weeds,
And drags behind a trail of chaos and death;
So burst we on that field, and through and through
The gay battalia brave with saffron silks,

Crushed and abolished every grace and gleam,
And dragged where'er we rode a sinuous track
Of chaos and death, till all the plain was filled
With battered armor, turbaned trunkless heads,
With silken mantles blushing angry gules
And Bagdad's banners trampled and forlorn.
And Saladin, stunned and bewildered sore, —
The greatest prince, save in the grace of God,
That now wears sword, — mounted his brother's barb,
And, followed by a half-score followers,
Sped to his castle Shaubec, over against
The cliffs by Ascalon, and there abode:
And sullenly made order that no more
The royal nouba should be played for him
Until he should erase the rusting stain
Upon his knightly honor; and no more
The nouba sounded by the Sultan's tent,

Morning nor evening by the silent tent,
Until the headlong greed of Chatillon
Spread ruin on our cause from Montreale.
But greatest are my warriors, as I deem,
In that their hearts, nearer than any else
Keep true the pledge of perfect purity
They pledged upon their sword-hilts long ago.
For all is possible to the pure in heart.

*Mother of God! thy starry smile*
  *Still bless us from above!*
*Keep pure our souls from passion's guile,*
  *Our hearts from earthly love!*
*Still save each soul from guilt apart*
  *As stainless as each sword,*
*And guard undimmed in every heart*
  *The image of our Lord!*

O goodliest fellowship that the world has known,
True hearts and stalwart arms! above your breasts
Glitters no flash of wreathen amulet
Forged against sword-stroke by the chanted rhythm
Of charms accurst; but in each steadfast heart
Blazes the light of cloudless purity,
That like a splendid jewel glorifies
With restless fire the gold that spheres it round,
And marks you children of our God, whose lives
He guards with the awful jealousy of love.
And even me that generous love has spared, —
Me, trustless knight and miserable man, —
Sad prey of dark and mutinous thoughts that tempt
My sick soul into perjury and death —
Since his great love had pity of my pain,
Has spared to lead these blameless warriors safe

Into the desert from the blazing towns,
Out of the desert to the inviolate hills
Where God has roofed them with his hollow shield.
Through all these days of tempest and eclipse
His hand has led me and his wrath has flashed
Its lightnings in the pathway of my sword.
And so I hope, and so my crescent faith
Gains daily power, that all my prayers and tears
And toils and blood and anguish borne for him
May blot the accusing of my deadly sin
From heaven's high compt, and give me rest in death;
And lay the pallid ghost of mortal love,
That fills with banned and mournful loveliness,
Unblest, the haunted chambers of my soul.
My misery will atone, — my misery, —

Dear God, will surely atone! for not the sting
Of macerating thongs, nor the slow horror
Of crowns of thorny iron maddening the brows,
Nor all that else pale hermits have devised
To scourge the rebel senses in their shade
Of caverned desolation, have the power
To smart and goad and lash and mortify
Like the great love that binds my ruined heart
Relentless, as the insidious ivy binds
The shattered bulk of some deserted tower,
Enlacing slow and riving with strong hands
Of pitiless verdure every seam and jut,
Till none may tear it forth and save the tower.
So binds and masters me my hopeless love.
So through the desert, in the silent hills,
I' the current of the battle's storm and stress,
One thought has driven me, — that though men may call

Me stainless Paladin, Knight leal and true
To Christ and Our Lady, still I know myself
A knight not after God's own heart, a soul
Recreant, and whelmed in the forbidden sin.
For dearer to my sad heart than the cross
I give my heart's best blood for are the eyes
That long ago, when youth and hope were mine,
I loved in thy still valleys, far Provence!
And sweeter to my spirit than the bells
Of rescued Salem are the loving tones
Of her dear voice, soft echoing o'er the years.
They haunt me in the stillness and the glare
Of desert noontide when the horizon's line
Swims faintly throbbing, and my shadow hides
Skulking beneath me from the brassy sky.
And when night comes to soothe with breath of
    balm

And pomp of stars the worn and weary world,
Her eyes rise in my soul and make its day.
And even into the battle comes my love,
Snatching the duty that I offer Heaven.

 At closing of El-Majed's awful day,
When the last quivering sunbeams, choked with dust
And fume of blood, failed on the level plain,
In the last charge, when gathered all our knights
The precious handful who from morn had stemmed
The fury of the multitudinous hosts
Of Islam, where in youth's hot fire and pride
Ramped the young lion-whelp, Ben-Saladin;
As down the slope we rode at eventide,
The dying sunlight faintly smiled to greet
Our tattered guidons and our dinted helms
And lance-heads blooming with the battle's rose.
Into the vale, dusk with the shadow of death,

With silent lips and ringing mail we rode.

And something in the spirit of the hour,

Or fate, or memory, or sorrow, or sin,

Or love, which unto me is all of these,

Possessed and bound me ; for when dashed our troop

In stormy clangor on the Paynim lines

The soul of my dead youth came into me ;

Faded away my oath ; the woes of Zion,

God was forgot ; blazed in my leaping heart,

With instant flash, life's inextinguished fires ;

Plunging along each tense limb poured the blood

Hot with its years of sleeping-smothered flame.

And in a dream I charged, and in a dream

I smote resistless ; foemen in my path

Fell unregarded, like the wayside flowers

Clipped by the truant's staff in daisied lanes.

For over me burned lustrous the dear eyes

Of my beloved ; I strove as at a joust
To gain at end the guerdon of her smile.
And ever, as in the dense melee I dashed,
Her name burst from my lips, as lightning breaks
Out of the plunging wrack of summer storms.

O my lost love ! Bright o'er the waste of years —
That bliss and beauty shines upon my soul ;
As far beyond yon desert hangs the sun,
Gilding with tender beam the barren stretch
Of sands that intervene. In this still light
The old sweet memories glimmer back to me.
Fair summers of my youth, — the idle days
I wandered in the bosky coverts hid
In the dim woods that girt my ancient home ;
The blue young eyes I met and worshipped there ;
The love that growing turned those gloomy wilds

To faery dells, and filled the vernal air
With light that bathed the hills of Paradise;
The warm, long days of rapturous summer-time,
When through the forests thick and lush we strayed,
And love made our own sunshine in the shades.
And all things fair and graceful in the woods
I loved with liberal heart; the violets
Were dear for her dear eyes, the quiring birds
That caught the musical tremble of her voice.
O happy twilights in the leafy glooms!
When in the glowing dusk the winsome arts
And maiden graces that all day had kept
Us twain and separate melted away
In blushing silence, and my love was mine
Utterly, utterly, with clinging arms
And quick, caressing fingers, warm red lips,
Where vows, half uttered, drowned in kisses, died;

Mine, with the starlight in her passionate eyes;
The wild wind of the woodland breathing low
To wake the elfin music of the leaves,
And free the prisoned odors of the flowers,
In honor of young Love come to his throne!
While we under the stars, with twining arms
And mutual lips insatiate, gave our souls —
Madly forgetting earth and héaven — to love!

*In desert march or battle's flame,*
 *In fortress and in field,*
*Our war-cry is thy holy name,*
 *Thy love our joy and shield!*
*And if we falter, let thy power*
 *Thy stern avenger be,*
*And God forget us in the hour*
 *We cease to think of thee!*

Curse me not, God of Justice and of Love!
Pitiful God, let my long woe atone!

I cannot deem but God has pitied me;
Else why with painful care have I been saved,
Whenever tossed and drenched in the fierce tide
Of Saladin's victories by the walls profaned
Of Jaffa, on the sands of far Daroum,
Or in the battle thundering on the downs
Of Ramlah, or the bloody day that shed
Red horrors on high Gaza's parapets?
For never a storm of fatal fight has raged
In Islam's track of rout and ruin swept
From Egypt to Gebail, but when the ebb
Of battle came I and my host have lain,
Scarred, scorched, safe somewhere on its fiery shore.
At Marcab's lingering siege, where day by day

We told the Moslem legions toiling slow,
Planting their engines, delving in their mines
To quench in our destruction this last light
Of Christendom, our fortress in the crags,
God's beacon swung defiant from the stars;
One thunderous night I knew their miners grop
Below, and thought ere morn to die, in crush
And tumult of the falling citadel.
And pondering of my fate — the broken storm
Sobbing its life away — I was aware
There grew between me and the quieting skies
A face and form I knew, — not as in dreams,
The sad dishevelled loveliness of earth,
But lighter than the thin air where she swayed,
Gold hair flame-fluttered, eyes and mouth aglow
With lambent light of spiritual joy.
With sweet command she beckoned me away

And led me vaguely dreaming, till I saw
Where the wild flood in sudden fury had burst
A passage through the rocks: and thence I led
My host unharmed, following her luminous eyes,
Until the East was gray, and with a smile
Wooing me heavenward still she passed away
Into the rosy trouble of the dawn.

And I believe my love is shrived in heaven,
And I believe that I shall soon be free.

For ever, as I journey on, to me
Waking or sleeping come faint whisperings
And fancies not of earth, as if the gates
Of near eternity stood for me ajar,
And ghostly gales come blowing o'er my soul
Fraught with the amaranth odors of the skies.
I go to join the Lion-Heart at Acre,

And there, after due homage to my liege,

And after patient penance of the church,

And after final devoir in the fight,

If that my God be gracious, I shall die.

And so I pray — Lord pardon if I sin! —

That I may lose in death's imbittered wave,

The stain of sinful loving, and may find

In glory again the love I lost below,

With all of fair and bright and unattained,

Beautiful in the cherishing smile of God,

By the glad waters of the River of Life!


Night hangs above the valley; dies the day

In peace, casting his last glance on my cross,

And warns me to my prayers. *Ave Maria!*

*Mother of God! the evening fades*
*On wave and hill and lea,*

*And in the twilight's deepening shades*
  *We lift our souls to thee!*
*In passion's stress — the battle's strife,*
  *The desert's lurking harms,*
*Maid-Mother of the Lord of Life,*
  *Protect thy men-at-arms!*

THE END.

---

Cambridge: Electrotyped and Printed by Welch, Bigelow, & Co.

www.ingramcontent.com/pod-product-compliance
Lightning Source LLC
Chambersburg PA
CBHW030245170426
43202CB00009B/636